C O R N

A COUNTRY GARDEN COOKBOOK

CORN

A COUNTRY GARDEN COOKBOOK

By David Tanis

Photography by Deborah Jones

CollinsPublishersSanFrancisco

A Division of HarperCollinsPublishers

First published in USA 1995 by Collins Publishers San Francisco
Copyright © 1995 by Collins Publishers San Francisco
Recipes and text copyright © 1995 David Tanis
Photographs copyright © 1995 Deborah Jones
Food Stylist: Sandra Cook
Floral and Prop Stylist: Sara Slavin
Art Direction and Design: Jennifer Barry
Series Editor: Meesha Halm
The corn illustration on page 45 is from The Best of the Old Farmer's
Almanac by Will Forpe. Copyright © 1977 by Jonathan David Publishers.
Reprinted with the permission of Jonathan David Publishers.
Library of Congress Cataloging-in-Publication Data
Tanis, David
Corn: a country garden cookbook/by David Tanis;
photography by Deborah Jones.
p.   cm.
Includes index.
ISBN 0-00-255450-X
1. Cookery (Corn)   I. Title.
TX809.M2T36 1995
641.6'567—dc20
CIP 94-39172

Printed in China
1 3 5 7 9 10 8 6 4 2

Acknowledgments

I'd like to thank the following cooks, farmers, associates, teachers and friends: Alice Waters, Niloufer Ichaporia, Catherine Brandel, Peggy Smith, Michael Wild, Brian Knox, Christine Galvin, Lili Lecocq, Elizabeth Berry, Randal Breski, Josephine Rooney, L.K. Larsen, Barbara Tanis, Bill Fujimoto, Joseph P. Guth, Tom Bruce, Mark Sanchez, Deborah Madison, Ernst Reck, Bob Cannard, Jenny Barry, Meesha Halm and the excellent staffs at Cafe Escalera and Chez Panisse.

Collins Publishers and the photography team would like to thank: Jeri Jones and Helga Sigvaldadottir, photo assistants; Allyson Levy, food styling assistant; Zonal and Naomi's of San Francisco, props; Assumpta Curry, design and production coordinator; and Susan Swant, manufacturing manager. Also to Dragon Fly Farm and Westside Farms in Healdsburg for their donation of produce and their farms for location photography. Special thanks to J. Carrie Brown and Charles Brown for allowing the location photography to be shot at the Jimtown Store in Healdsburg, CA.

CONTENTS

INTRODUCTION

Its scientific name is *Zea mays*. We North Americans call it corn, a habit that can be traced to a time when the English-speaking world referred to any grain or kernel as *corn*. The British, however, now call it *maize*. In Spanish it is *maíz*, from the Nahuatl word *mahiz*, which is how Columbus was introduced to it in the New World.

Although corn has been a staple grain throughout the Americas since long before the United States was founded, most modern North Americans think of corn, along with Mom and apple pie, with a fierce and loyal nostalgia, as a sort of basic birthright. We all have some vague notion of corn's place in pre-Columbian civilization or the corn lessons learned at Plymouth Rock, but many of us would be surprised to learn that the history of corn stretches back some 7,000 years. Probably descended from a wild grass in what is now southern Mexico—the exact botanical ancestry is uncertain—the five major classes of corn we know today (flint, flour, dent, pop and sweet) had already been developed by Native American farmers when the conquistadors arrived. Modern varieties of corn have been bred to produce and retain greater quantities of sugar, but the sweet corn we eat today is a mutation of Native American field corn, which was considerably less sweet and tender.

Today corn figures prominently in the hearts of cooks and diners throughout the world, having been incorporated into the cuisines of the East, West, North and South. But Mexico still heads the list in both the number and inventiveness of its corn dishes. The corn tortilla is ubiquitous and is an integral part of the culture. And there are wonderful tamales available in the most surprising places—one of the best I've ever eaten was bought through a train window and had a filling of squash blossoms and herbs. Perhaps the pinnacle of the Mexican corn experience is *huitlacoche,* the prized corn fungus, also known as corn smut, which looks evil but tastes divine and is sometimes compared to truffles. When picked fresh and cooked properly, it is delicious wrapped in a warm tortilla or scrambled with eggs. It is the sheer essence of corn.

Circling the globe, we find cornmeal dumplings and crêpes in parts of France, corn and shrimp soup in Thailand, fresh corn breads in India, fried corn bread in Portugal, and *mamaliga* in Romania. And who can imagine Italian cooking without polenta, the cornmeal staple of the north? In its simplest form, carefully stirred in a copper pot, then poured out in a golden circle, it is a humble peasant meal. Paired with long-simmered stews, baked with tomatoes and herbs or grilled with vegetables, it becomes sublime. I know a restaurant in Rome that, in addition to its regular menu, offers a separate menu entitled Polenta Fantasies.

In the United States regional corn cooking ranges from the scalloped corn and Indian puddings of the Northeast to the corn cakes and hominy grits of the South to the blue corn and *posole* of the Southwest. Hopi women still bake traditional waferlike corn-based *piki* bread on hot stones.

As a city-dwelling Midwesterner growing up in the 1950s, I share postmodern corn memories with others of my generation. I remember the little copper-bottomed Paul Revere saucepan it used to cook in, the whole frozen chunk tossed into an inch of boiling water and cooked for precisely twelve minutes. And I can still see the label rotating as a can of creamed corn was opened with an electric can opener. In summer, though, we always had fresh corn on the cob, making trips to the farm stand and rummaging through piles of corn in search of the plumpest ears.

Thankfully, we are experiencing a nationwide revolution in eating habits. Home gardening is once again becoming commonplace. Interest in heirloom varieties is increasing, as is an understanding of the importance of organic produce. As a result we are eating vegetables that are fresher and more flavorful. With corn, which deteriorates rapidly once picked—its sugars begin to turn to starch—this is especially critical. Nothing beats a couple of ears harvested from one's own garden and rushed to the cooking pot.

If you don't have a garden, local farmers' markets are a good solution. These markets offer social benefits as well. In the twentieth century our opportunities for conversation and exchanging ideas have diminished. Sometimes the best thing about the market is the chance to make human contact, to see the people who grew the vegetables, and to admire their perseverance in bringing them to town. Last year at the Santa Fe market I wandered by a truckload of freshly harvested corn. "Is this corn sweet?" I asked the white-haired overall-clad farmer. "Is honey?" he replied.

GLOSSARY

Although thousands of varieties of corn are available, corn is, after all, corn, and most varieties are interchangeable. Any type of corn can be popped, ground into meal, roasted, eaten fresh in the "milk" stage or made into porridge. However, over the course of 7,000 years, corn farmers have developed hybrids and strains of corn to satisfy a myriad of tastes and functions. A glimpse into a single seed catalog will reveal dozens of varieties available for planting, from exotic popcorns and Indian corn to the new Super Sweet types.

Most of the recipes in this book call for fresh sweet corn. They can be made with either white, yellow or bicolor kernels. You can substitute frozen corn, but the flavor will usually be compromised.

Although a diet of corn alone is not advisable, corn is wonderfully wholesome, especially when combined with other foods. Corn is high in vitamins, fiber and complex carbohydrates, but is incomplete as a protein. Corn is at its nutritional best when paired with dairy products, eggs or meat. Native Americans intuitively learned long ago to cook corn, squash and beans together, a combination that we now know yields a mutually beneficial set of amino acids.

Availability: Sweet corn is available only in summer. In most of the country, corn appears in July, but exactly when depends on where you live and what varieties are grown in your area. In California, Arizona and Texas, corn is available earlier. At higher elevations and in northern states, local corn may not come to market until late August. Certain varieties, such as Earlivee and Early Sunglow, are bred to bear early in the season; others, such as Silver Queen and Kandy Korn, bear at summer's end.

While it's true you may see corn in the supermarket at other times of the year—most of it from Florida, southern California and Mexico—it will usually not be of the best quality. The supermarket is not the best place to get corn in any case, since, ideally, corn should be cooked and eaten within minutes, or at least hours, of being picked. The best place to get corn is from your own or a friend's garden. Otherwise go to a roadside farm stand or a local produce market and ask if the corn was delivered that day. It is an extra effort—but the taste will be your reward.

Selecting: Look for an ear that is plump and green, with very fresh-looking husks and leaves and slightly sticky brown silk. Peel back a little bit of the husk to check that the kernels are firm, shiny, tightly spaced and free of decay and worm infestation. (Do not buy pre-shucked corn.)

In the field, wait to pick corn until the silk has dried and turned brown. With your thumbnail, pierce a kernel. If the juice is milky and sweet, the corn is ready. As the saying goes, you can stroll out to the corn patch, but run back! Have a pot of boiling water waiting.

Storing: If you must store corn, wrap it in a damp towel, then put it in a plastic bag and refrigerate for no more than two days. It will stay fresh but will lose sweetness, as corn's sugars begin turning to starch within minutes of picking. Super

Sweet varieties may be refrigerated for a week or more without losing sweetness, although they will lose some of their just-picked taste.

For long-term storage, remove the husks and boil or steam the corn on the cob for 2 minutes. Cool under running water and pat dry. Remove the kernels with a sharp knife, transfer to freezer bags and freeze for up to 6 months. Home-processed corn tastes much better than commercially-processed corn and is well worth the effort. Consult a standard technical cookbook for proper canning directions.

Preparing: Do not shuck corn until you are ready to cook since the husk keeps the corn from drying out. Kitchenware stores and seed catalogs offer a number of corn-related gadgets such as kernel-cutting devices (used for fresh, not cooked, ears) and de-silking brushes, which can be helpful if you are processing a lot of corn. If you have only a few ears, remove the husk by peeling from the silk end to the stem end and cut the ear in half crosswise. Brush the husked ear briskly with a dry towel to remove the silk. Stand the halved ear cut side down on a cutting board so that it rests firmly. Carefully cut the kernels from the cob with a sharp, serrated knife. One large ear yields approximately 1/2 cup kernels.

Cooking: Do try to use fresh corn if possible. Frozen corn is acceptable for longer-cooked dishes like stews and casseroles, but fresh is definitely preferred for salads and salsas. Above all, when cooking corn on the cob, be careful not to overcook it. Tender young sweet corn usually needs no more than 2 minutes in rapidly boiling unsalted water.

Growing Your Own Corn: The main requirements for growing corn are warm temperature, plenty of water and sufficient fertilizer. Consult a seed catalog or your County Extension Agent to pick varieties that grow well in your climate zone. If you plan to grow corn for eating fresh, your choice will probably fall on sweet corn. One of the advantages of opting for open-pollinated sweet corn is that it does not mature all at once like hybrid corn, so an extended harvest is possible. Ask your County Extension Agent about isolating varieties to avoid unwanted cross-pollination.

To plant, wait until the danger of frost is past and the weather is warm at night. Corn does not germinate well in cool soil. Prepare the soil with plenty of compost or manure. Sow seeds approximately 1 inch deep and approximately 1 foot apart, leaving 3 feet between the rows. Fertilize at planting time, when the plants are 8 inches tall, and again when they are 18 inches tall, using a fish emulsion or other high-nitrogen organic fertilizer. Do not let the soil dry out, especially when the ears are forming. Each stalk will bear one or two ears.

Seed Sources:

Nichols Garden Nursery
1190 North Pacific Highway
Albany, Oregon 97231-4598

Seed Savers Exchange
3076 North Winn Road
Decorah, Iowa 52101

Seeds of Change
P.O. Box 15700
Santa Fe, New Mexico
87506-5700

Shepherd's Garden Seeds
30 Irene Street
Torrington, Connecticut
06790

The Five Classes of Corn: There are five main classes of corn—dent, flint, flour, pop and sweet—as well as waxy corn, which is produced mostly for the cornstarch industry, and pod corn, which is an ancient primitive corn grown only for scientific research and for its unusual appearance (each kernel has a husk).

Dent corn *(also known as field corn)*: So called because of the small indentation in the top of the kernel when dry, dent corn is mostly yellow or white. Used mainly for livestock feed, it is the most widely cultivated corn in the United States. It is also used for cornmeal, oil and for a variety of industrial products, including ethanol, plastic bags and laundry starch. Best used for roasting, grinding, grits and cornmeal. *Hickory King* is an old-fashioned variety of dent corn.

Flint corn *(also known as Indian corn)*: Although quite edible, flint corn is usually grown for decorative purposes. It has hard kernels that range in color from white to red and is best ground into cornmeal. It is cultivated throughout the United States, especially in the Midwest. Varieties include *Rupp Indian Corn* and *Black Aztec*. It can be eaten fresh in the "milk" stage, when the kernels are opalescent. Allowed to dry, the kernels turn colors and can be ground into meal.

Flour corn: Cultivated in the southwestern United States, this corn is made up of primarily soft starches. It is most commonly ground to make into flour and cornmeal. It ranges in color from white to blue-gray to red and purple. Traditional southwestern strains include *Hopi Blue, Navajo Blue* and *Cochiti Blue*. They are used for blue corn flour and cornmeal and for making blue corn tortillas.

Popcorn: Cultivated throughout the United States, popcorn has small, hard kernels with a softer starch inside. When heated, the moisture in the soft starch begins to expand, and steam and pressure builds up, causing the unyielding hard starch on the exterior to explode, leaving behind a puff of starch and protein. Its main use is for popping, but many varieties are also grown for decorative purposes. It ranges in color from brown and black calico to strawberry red. Popcorn was probably the type of corn the ancient Native Americans used, both for grinding and popping. Popular varieties include *Burpee's Peppy, Pretty Pops* and *Strawberry*.

Sweet corn: The most familiar class of corn, this is the kind that comes to the market for corn on the cob and for other fresh uses. Sweet corn comes in yellow, white, bicolored and multicolored ears. It is harvested green, that is, before the kernels mature. There are two main types: open-pollinated sweet corn and hybrid sweet corn.

Open-pollinated sweet corn: This is the old-fashioned pure strain of corn our grandparents grew. It has not been improved or altered genetically. Some think it has a better flavor than hybrid corn. It must be eaten soon after picking. Varieties include *Country Gentleman,* which is an old heirloom variety producing uneven, "shoe-peg" kernels that are large, white and flavorful, and *Golden Bantam,* which is one of the first sweet corn types developed in modern horticulture. This yellow corn is a favorite of home gardeners.

Hybrid sweet corn: A cross of two genetically different strains, hybrid sweet corn is divided into three main groups: SU Hybrids, SH2 Hybrids and SE Hybrids. Although many people are enamored with the new sweeter hybrids—the SH2 Hybrids and SE Hybrids—for me, some are just too sweet. I'm not convinced that altering sugar genes has produced a superior product, even though it has resulted in improved shelf life. If you don't like your corn so sweet, be sure to ask what kind you are buying—you won't be able to tell what kind of hybrid it is just by looking.

SU Hybrids *(also called Normal Sugary)***:** These types of corn have a good, traditional corn flavor. They must be eaten soon after picking. Varieties include the yellow *Earlivee* and *Golden Beauty,* the white *Platinum Lady* and *White Lady,* the bicolored *Peaches and Cream* and the multicolored *Delectable,*

Triple Play and *Rainbow Inca,* as well as the following:

Early Sunglow: This yellow corn is ready only 62 days after planting. Ears are smaller than average, but sweet and tender.

Silver Queen: A wonderful white corn with delicious flavor, Silver Queen takes over three months to ripen. Its many fans agree it is worth the wait.

SH2 Hybrids *(also called Super Sweet or Shrunken):* These hybrids have been bred for a high sugar content and a crisp texture. The ears stay sweet for more than a week after picking. Varieties include *How Sweet It Is SH2,* a white Super Sweet containing two to three times the sugar of ordinary sweet corn, *Early Extra-Sweet SH2,* a large-eared yellow Super Sweet with very tender kernels, and *Candy Store SH2,* a bicolored ear for those who like Super Sweet but cannot decide between white and yellow.

SE Hybrids *(also known as EH Hybrids or Sugary Enhanced):* These hybrids have a high sugar content and a creamy texture and stay sweet long after harvesting.

Kandy Korn SE: This yellow corn is very sweet and creamy; it grows on burgundy stalks and has red-striped husks.

Seneca White Knight SE: This white corn variety has small, pearl-like kernels.

Miniature corn *(also known as Baby Corn):* These tiny ears are often sold canned and used in Chinese restaurants. Although most miniature corn is harvested from sweet corn, if you are growing corn, any variety can be harvested as baby corn. Simply pick it five days after the silk appears. Peel carefully to reveal a tiny but perfectly formed ear about 3 inches long. The whole ear is edible.

Dried Corn Products:

Chicos: Found in New Mexico, chicos are ears of corn that are steamed or roasted and dried. The kernels are then removed and cooked with pork, beef or beans for a hearty stew.

Cornmeal: Although it can be made from any variety of dried corn, cornmeal is usually ground from yellow or white dent corn. In the United States it is commonly used for corn bread, pancakes and mush. Italian polenta is usually made from a yellow cornmeal that comes either coarsely or finely ground. When purchasing cornmeal, look for stone-ground, natural products. They will have more corn flavor than the degerminated cornmeal available in supermarkets.

Hominy: Known in Spanish as *posole,* this dried, hulled field corn is common throughout Mexico and the American Southwest. Early Native Americans discovered that soaking dried corn in water with wood ashes helped remove the outer hulls from the kernels. Today a mild slaked-lime solution accomplishes the same task. Hominy was once a staple pantry item in most American homes, but now is considered old-fashioned. It is still found in southern states, but more popular are hominy grits, which are made from dried, ground hominy meal and cooked into a kind of porridge.

Masa harina: Used for tortillas and tamales, this flour is made from finely ground lime-treated corn. Most supermarkets carry Quaker brand instant *masa harina,* but you can buy a superior ready-made *masa* (dough) in Mexican grocery stores.

Burpee's Peppy

Silver Queen

Pretty Pops

Rainbow Inca

Early Sunglow

Delectable

How Sweet It Is SH2

Candy Store SH2

Miniature Corn

Rupp Indian Corn

OPENERS

Whether they are casual snacks with drinks or the formal first course at a sit-down dinner, openers must stimulate the taste buds and please the eye. Corn certainly satisfies these requirements. Brightly colored kernels lend a festive look to almost any dish. Corn has great versatility, too. Its natural sweetness pairs well with other sweet flavors, such as grilled onions and peppers. But corn is equally at home with chile, lime and cilantro—great tastes to awaken a dulled palate.

Cornmeal Blini with Smoked Salmon and Crème Fraîche make an elegant opener with a glass of champagne. A duet of corn soups offers distinct personalities that can match any occasion: the Roasted White Corn Chowder with Garlic and Herb Butter is deep and savory and the White Corn and Roasted Pepper Soup is smooth and velvety. For those really sweltering days, try the summer salads with corn, which are mouthwatering and easy to prepare.

The East Indian–inspired corn dishes—spicy popcorn, a creamy raita and Grilled Lamb Skewers with Corn Chutney—could be the prelude to a banquet or the basis for a spicy outdoor lunch. At the other end of the spectrum is the corn and goat cheese pudding, which is rich and impressive. And good old corn on the cob is everything an opener should be…immediate, flavorful and hands-on!

Spicy Bombay Popcorn

Once you try popcorn this way, you may never return to the plain old stuff.
Vary the amount of cayenne to suit the taste of the group, but keep it spicy!

4 tablespoons vegetable oil
1/2 cup popcorn
1 tablespoon cumin seed
1 tablespoon whole black peppercorns
1 tablespoon coriander seed
1/2 teaspoon whole allspice
6 whole cloves

4 tablespoons (1/2 stick) unsalted butter
1/2 teaspoon cayenne, or to taste
1 teaspoon powdered turmeric
1 teaspoon finely chopped garlic
1 teaspoon grated fresh ginger
Sea salt, to taste

In a large, heavy-bottomed pot with a lid, heat the oil over medium heat. Add the popcorn, stir well to coat with oil and cover with the lid. Shake the pot for 3 to 4 minutes, or until you hear that the corn has popped. Alternatively, if you are using an electric corn popper or air popper, follow the manufacturer's directions.

Heat a dry skillet over medium heat. Add the cumin, peppercorns, coriander, allspice and cloves. Shake the pan until the spices color slightly and smell toasted, about 1 minute. Transfer the spices to an electric spice mill or mortar and pestle and grind to a coarse powder.

In the same skillet, melt the butter over low heat. Stir in the toasted ground spices, the cayenne, turmeric, garlic and ginger. Pour the flavored butter over the popped corn and toss well. Add sea salt to taste and mix again. Serve warm in a brightly colored bowl. *Makes 12 cups; serves 4 to 6*

Grilled Lamb Skewers with Corn Chutney

Make the skewers very small for cocktails, or double the recipe for a picnic supper. The corn chutney, which is best the day it is made, is also an excellent foil for lamb chops or roast lamb. You can find the garam masala spice mix in Indian and specialty grocery shops.

Corn Chutney:
Kernels from 2 large ears sweet corn (or 1 cup frozen corn, thawed)
2 cups firmly packed cilantro, coarsely chopped
1/4 cup packed fresh mint
2 jalapeño peppers, sliced 1/8 inch thick
2 tablespoons coarsely chopped fresh ginger
1 teaspoon granulated sugar
1/2 cup cold water
Salt and freshly ground black pepper, to taste
Juice of 1 large lime

1 pound ground lean lamb
1 teaspoon coriander seed
1 teaspoon cumin seed
1/4 teaspoon cayenne
1/2 teaspoon garam masala
4 cloves garlic, finely chopped
2 tablespoons finely chopped fresh ginger
1 teaspoon salt
1 egg, lightly beaten
1 package 8-inch-long bamboo skewers
Lettuce leaves, for lining platter
1 bunch cilantro and 2 limes, for garnish

In a food processor fitted with the metal blade, process all the chutney ingredients, pulsing on and off until the mixture is slightly chunky. Season with additional salt or lime juice, if necessary. Cover and refrigerate.

Preheat the broiler or prepare a grill.

Put the ground lamb in a large mixing bowl. In a dry skillet, toast the coriander and cumin seeds over medium heat for approximately 1 minute, or until slightly brown and aromatic. Grind them in an electric spice mill or with a mortar and pestle, then sprinkle over the lamb. Add the cayenne, garam masala, garlic, ginger, salt and egg and mix well. Divide

the meat mixture into 8 pieces (or more, for very small skewers). With wet hands, form the meat mixture into long sausage shapes, approximately 3/4 inch in diameter, around the bamboo skewers, leaving approximately 1 inch free at the bottom of the skewer as a handle. Grill the skewers under the broiler or over coals for approximately 5 minutes, turning once.

To serve, line a large platter with lettuce leaves. Put the chutney in a decorative bowl in the center of the platter. Arrange the hot skewers around the chutney and garnish with the lime, cut in wedges, and sprigs of cilantro.
Serves 4

Fresh Corn Raita with Pappadams

*Served with cool drinks, such as beer and gin and tonics, this makes a wonderful snack
on a hot day. Toasting rather than frying the pappadams—traditional chickpea wafers—keeps
the dish light. The raita is also a great sauce for grilled fish.*

1 quart plain unsweetened yogurt
2 large ears sweet corn (or 1 cup frozen corn, thawed)
2 tablespoons vegetable oil or clarified butter
    (also known as ghee)
1 tablespoon black mustard seed
1 tablespoon cumin seed
1 tablespoon finely chopped garlic
Salt, to taste

1 tablespoon finely chopped or grated fresh ginger
1 tablespoon finely chopped fresh mint
Pinch of cayenne
2 tablespoons roughly chopped fresh cilantro (optional)
1 jalapeño pepper, seeds and veins removed,
    finely chopped (optional)

1 package (200 grams) pappadams, available in
    Indian and specialty grocery stores

Using a rubber spatula, transfer the yogurt to a 2-quart mixing bowl. With a corn kernel remover or a sharp knife, cut the corn off the cob and place in a small bowl. Set aside.

Heat the oil in an 8-inch skillet over medium heat. Add the mustard and cumin seeds and shake the pan. The seeds will begin to pop and release their aroma. Turn the heat to low and add the garlic, being careful not to let it brown. Add the corn kernels and a little salt and stir well with a wooden spoon. Continue stirring over low heat for 2 minutes.

Transfer the contents of the skillet into the yogurt. (There will be a little sizzling and spattering.) Stir to incorporate the corn mixture, then add the ginger, mint, cayenne, and cilantro and jalapeño, if using. Mix well. Let sit for 10 minutes to allow the flavors to blend. Taste and add more salt, if necessary. If not serving immediately, allow the raita to cool and then refrigerate, covered, for up to 3 hours.

To crisp the pappadams, heat them one at a time in a toaster oven until they look bubbly. They may also be toasted over an open flame. To serve, pour the raita into a serving dish. Break the crisped pappadams into large pieces and place around the raita. Dip the pappadams into the raita as you would chips. *Serves 4 to 6*

Cornmeal Blini with Smoked Salmon and Crème Fraîche

This is a variation on the classic Russian buckwheat blini, and a real crowd-pleaser.
The dish can be miniaturized for cocktails: Pass a platter of tiny blini topped with caviar.

1/2 cup all-purpose unbleached flour
1/2 cup fine yellow cornmeal
2 teaspoons baking powder
1/2 teaspoon salt
3/4 cup milk
1 egg

2 tablespoons unsalted butter, melted
8 ounces sliced smoked salmon
1/2 cup crème fraîche or sour cream
Capers, pickled onions, nasturtium petals, freshly
    ground black pepper, red or black caviar or
    snipped chives, for toppings (optional)

Preheat the oven to the warm setting or 200 degrees F.

In a medium-sized mixing bowl, combine the flour, cornmeal, baking powder and salt. In a separate bowl, beat together the milk and egg, then pour over the flour mixture. Mix lightly to make a medium-thick pancake batter. If necessary, thin it with a little more milk. Stir in the melted butter.

Heat a nonstick frying pan or griddle or a lightly oiled cast-iron skillet over medium heat. Ladle in 2 tablespoons of batter for each pan-cake. Cook for approximately 2 minutes, or until the tops are bubbly, then flip and cook 1 minute more. Remove the cooked pancakes to an ovenproof dish and keep them in the warm oven until all the batter has been used.

Briefly warm 4 small plates in the oven.

To serve, put 3 or 4 blini on each warmed plate. Drape the salmon slices around the blini and dot the blini with a heaping tablespoon of crème fraîche. Garnish to taste with any, or all, of the suggested toppings. *Serves 4*

White Corn and Roasted Pepper Soup

This velvety puréed soup is like liquid summer. Be sure to peel the peppers carefully;
pepper skins can be bitter when puréed.

2 red bell peppers
2 yellow bell peppers
2 large yellow onions, finely diced
2 tablespoons light olive oil
Salt, to taste
4 or 5 cloves garlic, peeled
Kernels from 4 large ears sweet white corn (or 2 cups
*   frozen corn, thawed)*

2 large russet potatoes, finely diced
1 teaspoon fresh thyme
Freshly ground black pepper, to taste
6 cups unsalted chicken stock, heated
Pinch of cayenne
1/2 teaspoon red wine vinegar, or to taste
Chives, basil and 4 teaspoons crème fraîche, for
*   garnish (optional)*

Preheat the broiler or prepare a grill.

Place the bell peppers as close as possible to the heat and roast them, turning frequently with a pair of tongs, for approximately 5 minutes until the skins blacken and blister. Put the peppers in a paper bag and close the bag or cover with a towel for 5 minutes; they will steam a little and be easier to peel. To peel the peppers, cut them in half lengthwise and remove the stem and seeds with a paring knife or fingers. Scrape the charred skin off the flattened peppers with the knife. Do not rinse—water will dilute the flavor. If necessary, use a paper towel to remove any stubborn bits of skin or seed. Cut the peppers into 1/2-inch dice and set aside.

In a heavy-bottomed 3-quart pot over medium heat, sauté the onions in the olive oil. Salt lightly and allow them to brown slightly. Reduce the heat to low and, stirring occasionally, cook for approximately 10 minutes, or until the onions are soft. Add the garlic, corn,

potatoes and thyme and season with salt and pepper. Increase the heat to high, stir well and add 4 cups of the stock. When the soup comes to a hard boil, reduce the heat to a simmer and cook, uncovered, for 15 minutes, or until the potatoes are soft. Add three quarters of the roasted peppers to the soup, reserving the rest for garnish. Simmer for 5 minutes more.

In a blender, purée the soup in several batches. Strain the mixture through a wire sieve or conical strainer, pushing against the solids with a wooden spoon to extract all the liquid. Discard the solids. Reheat the soup over medium heat. Add the cayenne and a few drops of red wine vinegar. If necessary, thin the soup with a little more chicken stock. Taste for salt and pepper and adjust as necessary.

To serve, ladle the soup into 4 wide bowls. Sprinkle the reserved bell peppers on top. If desired, garnish with chives, torn basil leaves and a teaspoon of crème fraîche. *Serves 4*

Roasted White Corn Chowder with Garlic and Herb Butter

The problem with this soup is that no one wants dinner afterward—just more corn chowder. It's that good.

4 large ears sweet white corn (or 2 cups frozen corn, thawed)
Light olive or vegetable oil, for oiling corn
1 large yellow onion, finely diced
2 tablespoons light olive oil
2 leeks, washed well and finely diced (optional)
2 cups finely diced bell pepper (green, yellow or a combination)
1 jalapeño pepper, seeded and very finely chopped
1 sprig fresh thyme
1 bay leaf
Salt, to taste

3 to 4 potatoes, peeled and cut into small dice
4 cups unsalted chicken stock or water

Garlic and Herb Butter:
4 tablespoons unsalted butter, softened
1/2 teaspoon finely chopped garlic
1 tablespoon finely chopped fresh chives
1 tablespoon finely chopped fresh basil
1 tablespoon finely chopped Italian parsley
Juice and zest of 1 small lime
Pinch of cayenne
Salt and freshly ground black pepper, to taste

Prepare a bed of coals in a covered barbecue.

Shuck the corn, oil lightly and roast the whole ears, covered, for 10 to 15 minutes. Alternatively (or if using frozen corn), roast the corn beneath a gas broiler, turning occasionally, for approximately 10 minutes, or until slightly browned. Let cool. With a sharp knife, slice the kernels from the cob and set aside.

In a heavy-bottomed stockpot or Dutch oven, sauté the onion in the olive oil over medium heat for 5 or 6 minutes, or until it browns lightly. Add the leeks, if using, and let

them stew for 3 to 4 minutes. Add the bell pepper, jalapeño, thyme, bay leaf and salt and let the mixture stew for 2 or 3 minutes longer. Add the potatoes and chicken stock. Bring the soup to a hard boil, let boil for 2 minutes, then lower the heat and gently simmer for 10 minutes. Taste the broth and add salt if necessary. Add the reserved corn kernels and simmer for another 10 minutes until the potatoes are tender and the broth has thickened slightly. For a thicker version, purée 1 to 1 1/2 cups of the soup in a food processor or blender and stir back into the soup.

In a small bowl, using a wooden spoon, mash the butter with the garlic and herbs. Add the lime juice and zest, cayenne and salt and pepper to taste. With a rubber spatula, scrape the butter mixture onto a piece of waxed paper. Roll up into a rough cylinder and refrigerate for 10 minutes, so it will be easy to slice.

The soup may be served immediately or refrigerated for up to 4 hours and then gently reheated.

To serve, ladle the chowder into wide bowls. Float a 1/2-inch slice of the butter on each serving. *Serves 4*

Corn, Avocado, Jicama and Radish Salad

This salad has all the bright flavors of Mexico. The secret is to choose perfectly ripe, but not overripe, avocados. Make sure to have ice-cold beer and tortilla chips on hand.

Dressing:
1 teaspoon cumin seed
1/2 cup light olive oil
1 clove garlic, finely chopped
Juice and zest of 1 orange
Juice of 2 large limes
Large pinch of cayenne, or to taste
Salt and freshly ground black pepper, to taste
1 teaspoon paprika

1 small jicama or 1 small daikon radish
1 bunch small red radishes
*3 large ears sweet corn, boiled (see p. 43) and kernels
    removed (or 1 1/2 cups frozen corn, thawed)*
1/2 cup thinly sliced green onions
2 large ripe but firm avocados
2 teaspoons paprika
1/2 cup loosely packed cilantro

To prepare the dressing, place the cumin seeds in a dry skillet over medium heat and toast until slightly browned and aromatic. Remove from the heat and let cool. Grind the cumin seeds into a fine powder in an electric spice mill or with a mortar and pestle.

Pour the oil into a small bowl. Add the ground cumin to the olive oil, along with the garlic, orange juice and zest, lime juice, cayenne, salt, pepper and paprika. Mix lightly with a fork or whisk. Set aside.

Peel the jicama and slice 1/4 inch thick. Stack the slices into neat piles and cut the slices crosswise into 1/4-inch sticks. Slice the radishes into thin coin-shaped slices.

In a large bowl, combine the corn, jicama, radishes and green onions. Season to taste with salt and pepper. Pour the dressing over the vegetables, toss well and set aside for 10 minutes to allow the flavors to mingle.

Cut the avocados in half and remove the pits. Carefully pull off the skin so that the avocado flesh stays intact and unmarred. Now cut the halves into thin slices. Divide the avocados slices among 4 chilled salad plates. Toss the corn mixture again and spoon over and around the avocados. Sprinkle each salad with a large pinch of paprika. Scatter the cilantro leaves over the salads and serve immediately. *Serves 4*

Fresh Corn and Roasted Duck Tamales with Smoked Chile

*Tamales are great party food; they fill the house with tantalizing aromas, and the little
corn-husk packages are fun to open and eat. Be sure to keep the water boiling rapidly in the pot so
that the tamales will be tender—lower heat will make them stodgy.*

Filling:
6 duck legs (approximately 3 pounds), Long Island
   or Peking
Salt and freshly ground black pepper, to taste
6 tablespoons canned chipotle chile★
1 head garlic
1 lemon, quartered
8 cups unsalted chicken stock, homemade or canned,
   heated
1 large yellow onion, finely diced
2 tablespoons light olive oil or vegetable oil

4 large ears sweet corn (or 2 cups frozen corn,
   thawed)
1 tablespoon cumin seed
Juice of 1 small lime, or to taste

3 dozen dried corn husks★
1/2 cup lard or vegetable shortening
4 cups Quaker masa harina
1 teaspoon salt
1/2 teaspoon baking powder
2 to 2 1/2 cups homemade duck stock or unsalted
   chicken stock, homemade or canned, heated

Preheat the oven to 400 degrees F.

   Rinse the duck legs and pat them dry.
Season liberally with salt and pepper. Finely
chop the chipotle chile and set half aside; smear
the other half over the entire surface of the

duck legs. Place the duck legs in a Pyrex baking
dish or enameled casserole and add the whole
head of garlic, the lemon and the chicken stock.
Roast, uncovered, for 1 1/2 to 2 hours until the
meat is quite tender. An inserted fork or skewer

should come out easily and the juices should run clear. Remove the duck legs (reserving the cooking liquid) and leave to cool on a platter at room temperature.

In a 9-inch skillet, sauté the onion over medium heat in the oil. Salt lightly and cook approximately 5 minutes until translucent and lightly browned. Using a corn kernel remover or a sharp knife, cut the kernels from the ears of corn and add to the onions. Stir well and cook 1 minute longer. Transfer the corn mixture to a 3-quart mixing bowl.

In a dry skillet over medium-high heat, toast the cumin seed until it browns slightly. Grind in an electric spice mill or with a mortar and pestle and add to the corn mixture.

When the duck legs have cooled, remove and discard the skin and pick all the meat from the bones. Chop the meat roughly by hand into pieces slightly larger than the corn kernels. Add to the corn mixture. Add the remaining chipotle chile, 1 cup of the reserved cooking liquid and the lime juice. Mix well with a wooden spoon or spatula. Taste, then add salt and pepper, if necessary.

Place the dried corn husks in a large bowl of hot water for 20 to 30 minutes to soften.

To make the tamale dough, beat the lard in a large mixing bowl with an electric mixer until fluffy. Add the *masa harina,* salt and baking powder and mix well. Slowly add 2 cups of the heated stock and continue beating for 5 to 8 minutes until the mixture thickens to the consistency of mashed potatoes. If necessary, thin with up to 1/2 cup more stock and beat 2 minutes more.

When the corn husks are soft, drain them and pat dry to remove excess water. Cut or tear 8 of the husks lengthwise into 1/4-inch strips. For each tamale, flatten a corn husk and spread approximately 2 tablespoons of the tamale dough in the center of the husk. Put a tablespoon of the duck mixture on top of the dough and press it in lightly with your fingertips. Fold the filled husk like an envelope and wrap with a 1/4-inch strip of corn husk to secure, tying with a bow. Alternatively, roll the husk with filling lengthwise into a sausage shape and tie both ends with strips of husk.

Place a steamer rack in a large pot with a tight-fitting lid and fill with water until it reaches 1 inch below the rack. Remove the rack and bring the water to a boil. Line the steamer rack with the corn husks and place the tamales loosely inside. Place the steamer rack into the pot, cover and steam the tamales for approximately 1 1/2 hours. Add more boiling water as necessary to maintain a vigorous boil. Test one tamale to make sure the dough is fully cooked—it should be tender, not doughy— then serve the rest immediately. *Makes approximately 24 small tamales; serves 8 to 10*

★*Available in Mexican and some specialty groceries.*

Lobster and Arugula Salad with Corn Salsa

Lobster and corn seem to be made for each other and for the sunny flavors of summer. This salad is at once elegant and earthy—good for a fancy dinner or a lazy lunch at the beach.

2 tablespoons salt, plus more to taste
2 live lobsters, 1 1/2 pounds each (or 4 frozen baby
    lobster tails, thawed)
1/2 cup extra virgin olive oil
Juice of 1 lemon
3 tablespoons red wine vinegar
3 cloves garlic, finely chopped
3 large ears sweet corn, boiled (see p. 43) and kernels
    removed (or 1 1/2 cups frozen corn, thawed)
2 large ripe tomatoes, peeled, seeded and finely diced
1/2 cup finely diced red bell pepper

1/2 cup finely diced yellow bell pepper
2 jalapeño peppers, seeded, deveined and
    very finely chopped (optional)
1 small red onion, finely diced
1 tablespoon snipped fresh chives
1 teaspoon finely chopped fresh tarragon
1 tablespoon finely chopped Italian parsley
1 tablespoon finely chopped green or purple basil
Freshly ground black pepper, to taste
6 cups loosely packed arugula, or a mixture of
    spinach and watercress

In a large pot over high heat, bring 1 gallon of water to a rolling boil. Add the 2 tablespoons of salt and the lobsters, bring the water back to a boil and cook for 5 minutes. Remove the lobsters and let cool to room temperature. Crack the shells, remove the meat from the tails and claws and slice into 1/2-inch pieces.

In a large bowl, whisk together the oil, lemon juice, vinegar and garlic. Add the corn, tomato, bell peppers, jalapeños (if using), onion, chives, tarragon, parsley and basil. Season with salt and black pepper and mix lightly. Add the lobster slices and toss gently.

Wash the arugula and spin dry. Divide among 4 chilled salad plates. Spoon the lobster and salsa mixture over the arugula and serve at once. *Serves 4*

White Corn, Cherry Tomato and Yellow Pepper
Salad with Purple Basil

When the corn, tomatoes and peppers in the garden are at their peak in flavor, it is time to make this salad. Resist any temptation to make it out of season. You'll see why when you taste it.

4 large ears sweet white corn, such as White Lady
2 large yellow bell peppers
1 pound cherry tomatoes, such as Sweet 100, or an assortment of small tomatoes of varied colors

Vinaigrette:
1/2 cup extra virgin olive oil

2 tablespoons fresh lemon juice
2 tablespoons red wine vinegar
1 to 2 cloves garlic, finely chopped
2 to 3 green onions, thinly sliced

Salt and freshly ground black pepper, to taste
1/2 cup purple (or green) basil leaves

Over high heat, bring a large pot of water to a boil. Add the corn and cook for 2 minutes. Allow the corn to cool.

Preheat the broiler or prepare a grill.

Place the bell peppers as close as possible to the heat and roast them, turning frequently with a pair of tongs, for approximately 5 minutes until the skins blacken and blister. Put the peppers in a paper bag and close the bag or cover with a towel for 5 minutes; they will steam a little and be easier to peel. Cut them in half lengthwise and remove the stem and seeds with a paring knife or fingers. Scrape the flattened peppers with the knife to remove the charred skin. Do not rinse—water will dilute the flavor. If necessary, use a paper towel to remove any stubborn bits of skin or seed. Slice the peppers into 1/2-inch strips. (If you do not wish to roast and peel the peppers, you can use them raw, but slice as thinly as possible.)

Using a sharp knife, slice the corn kernels from the cob and place in a large, shallow porcelain salad bowl. Add the roasted peppers. Cut each tomato into halves or quarters and add to the bowl.

In a small bowl, mix together the oil, lemon juice, vinegar, garlic and green onions.

Salt and pepper the vegetables liberally, pour the vinaigrette over the top, toss gently and let sit for 10 minutes at room temperature.

If serving the salad from the bowl, toss gently once more, then garnish with torn and whole basil leaves. Alternatively, serve on individual plates. *Serves 4*

White Corn and Goat Cheese Pudding with Warm Mustard Greens and Pancetta

Not as difficult to execute as a soufflé, but just as appealing, this is a forgiving recipe.
A little more or less of one ingredient does not affect the outcome.

1 yellow onion, finely diced
3 tablespoons olive oil
4 large ears sweet white corn, preferably Silver
    Queen (or 2 cups frozen corn, thawed)
Salt and freshly ground black pepper, to taste
1 tablespoon chopped fresh thyme
2 tablespoons unsalted butter
2 tablespoons all-purpose unbleached flour
1 cup milk or half-and-half
Pinch of cayenne

2 eggs, separated
4 to 6 ounces mild goat cheese or fresh ricotta or
    cream cheese
6 tablespoons (2 ounces) freshly grated Parmesan cheese

4 ounces pancetta or smoked bacon, sliced into
    1/4-inch strips
2 cloves garlic, finely chopped
4 to 6 cups tender young mustard or turnip greens or
    spinach leaves, washed and drained

Preheat the oven to 350 degrees F. Butter a 1-quart casserole, soufflé or earthenware dish.

In a medium-sized skillet over low heat, gently sauté the onion in 1 tablespoon of the oil for 3 to 4 minutes until soft and barely golden. With a sharp knife, slice the kernels from the cob and add to the skillet. Add salt and pepper to taste and sauté for 2 minutes. Remove from the heat and stir in the thyme. Set aside.

In a heavy saucepan or skillet over low heat, melt the butter, being careful not to let it brown. Stir in the flour with a wooden spoon or whisk. Slowly add the milk, and stirring well, cook for approximately 5 minutes until smooth and thick. Still stirring, cook approximately 5 minutes longer. Remove from the heat. Season with salt, pepper and cayenne. Let cool slightly, then beat in the egg yolks one at a time. Add the corn mixture and stir well. Crumble in the goat cheese and mix lightly. Add half the grated Parmesan and mix again.

In a medium-sized bowl, beat the egg whites until stiff. Stir one-third of the beaten whites into the corn mixture, then fold in the remaining egg whites with a rubber spatula. Quickly pour the mixture into the prepared casserole. Sprinkle the top with the remaining Parmesan. Bake for 30 to 35 minutes until an inserted cake tester or table knife comes out clean. (If you do not plan to serve it straight away, the pudding can stand at room temperature for up to 2 hours and then be reheated.)

In a large, deep skillet, heat the remaining oil. Over medium heat, sauté the *pancetta* for 1 to 2 minutes until crisp. Add the garlic and stir, taking care not to let it brown. Add the greens, season with salt and pepper and stir for 1 to 2 minutes, or until barely wilted.

Divide the greens among individual plates, top with a large spoonful or wedge of the pudding and serve at once. *Serves 4 to 6*

Corn on the Cob

*Although eating fresh sweet corn, boiled briefly and devoured joyfully with butter
and salt, is an American ritual, here are some other options for corn on the cob for those willing
to break with tradition. Amounts are given per ear.*

Boiling:

If your corn is young, fresh and tender, remove the husks and cook it for a maximum of 2 minutes in rapidly boiling unsalted water in an uncovered pot. (Salted water makes the kernels tough.) Don't crowd the ears; cook no more than six at a time in a gallon of water. Serve immediately. Your guests should wait for the corn, not vice versa!

If your corn is a little older or has been refrigerated, boil it for five minutes and add 2 tablespoons of sugar to the water. This will help, but it won't make old corn young.

Mexican-Style Corn on the Cob:

1/2 cup salt
Ground dried red chile, preferably ancho or cayenne
1 lime, cut in half

In a small bowl, mix the salt and chile, making the mixture as spicy as you like. Dip the cut side of the lime into the salt-chile mixture and rub it down the length of an ear of cooked corn. Squeeze a little more lime juice over the corn.

Mediterranean-Style Corn on the Cob

Extra virgin olive oil, to taste
Sea salt and freshly ground black pepper, to taste
Hot red pepper flakes, to taste

Drizzle boiled or grilled corn with oil, then sprinkle with salt, pepper and red pepper flakes.

Grilling:

Everyone has a different method for grilling corn. One time-honored technique is to pull back the husks, remove the silk, tie the husks back on and soak the ears in cold water for twenty minutes. Grill the corn over hot coals, turning occasionally, for 15 to 20 minutes. This method steams the corn inside the husk, and the charred husk perfumes the corn as well.

Another method is to shuck the corn completely, oil lightly, then roast it in a covered barbecue for 10 to 15 minutes, turning occasionally.

Jalapeño and Cumin Butter:

1 tablespoon unsalted butter, softened
1/4 teaspoon finely chopped fresh or pickled jalapeños
1/4 teaspoon cumin seed, toasted, then ground
1 teaspoon chopped cilantro

Sage and Chive Butter:

1 tablespoon unsalted butter, softened
1/4 teaspoon finely chopped fresh sage
1/4 teaspoon finely chopped fresh chives
1/2 teaspoon fresh lemon juice

Dill and Chervil Butter:

1 tablespoon unsalted butter, softened
1/4 teaspoon finely chopped fresh dill
1/4 teaspoon finely chopped fresh chervil or parsley
Freshly ground black pepper, to taste

In a small bowl, mix the butter with the preferred flavorings. Spread liberally on the corn.

ACCOMPANIMENTS

Corn, with its sweet flavor, is a natural partner to the main course. It marries especially well with roasted or grilled meats. Try the "Improved" Creamed Corn, which is dressed up with southwestern flair, the next time you grill pork chops. Or pair the Corn and Potato Gratin with a garlicky steak.

The cornmeal-based dishes, which are completely addicting, are designed as side dishes. Served warm from the oven, they can accompany anything from a juicy roasted chicken to pan-fried catfish. Who wouldn't welcome a warm slice of corn bread, crunchy corn fritters or a golden spoonful of corn bread stuffing? Buy the best natural, fresh-milled cornmeal you can find from health-food stores, gourmet shops or Italian delicatessens. The recipes will work with supermarket-type cornmeal, but you'll get more flavor and nutrients from better-quality brands.

Other dishes, like the Native American Stew and the paella-like Baked Saffron Rice, could be meals in themselves —simply increase the portion sizes. Served with a green salad, grilled polenta makes a terrific light lunch. In fact, polenta is one of the world's most versatile grain dishes. A bowl of soft polenta with a little butter and Parmesan cheese or brown sugar and heavy cream makes a comfort food without rival. Finally, I hope that the Spontaneous Succotash will inspire you to overcome any residual childhood fear of lima beans.

Savory Corn Custard

This dish is easy to make, but guests will be impressed, nonetheless. The combination of corn,
saffron and green onion is quite delicate suspended in a silky egg custard. Try it as an unusual breakfast treat,
or serve as a side dish with something that won't overpower it, such as a simple grilled chicken breast.

2 tablespoons unsalted butter
Kernels from 3 large ears white corn (or 1 1/2 cups
  frozen corn, thawed)
Salt and freshly ground black pepper, to taste

1/2 cup thinly sliced green onions
2 eggs
1 cup half-and-half
1/8 teaspoon Spanish saffron, crumbled

Preheat the oven to 375 degrees F.

In a 10-inch sauté pan, melt the butter over low heat. Add the corn kernels and increase the heat to medium and gently warm the corn through, approximately 2 minutes. Remove from heat.

Season with salt and pepper and stir to distribute equally. Spoon the corn kernels into a 1 1/2-quart soufflé dish or divide evenly among 4 individual soufflé dishes. Sprinkle the green onions over the corn.

In a small bowl, whisk together the eggs and the half-and-half. Add the saffron and a large pinch of salt and whisk together again.

Pour the egg mixture over the corn. Place the soufflé dish(es) in a deep-sided roasting pan and add boiling water to a depth of 2 inches. Cover the pan tightly with aluminum foil, enclosing the dish(es). Place the pan on the middle shelf of the oven and bake for 30 minutes, or until the custard is just set. The surface will be firm but wiggly; a small, sharp knife when inserted in the center should come out clean. Remove the soufflé(s) carefully from the hot-water bath. Serve individual custards in their dishes with teaspoons. Serve the larger custard at the table, giving each guest a large spoonful. *Serves 4*

Spoon Bread

*A southern favorite, spoon bread is a cross
between corn bread and a pudding, meant to be
served alongside meat. Like mashed potatoes,
spoon bread is especially good with gravy.*

2 cups water
1 cup fine white cornmeal
Kernels from 2 large ears white corn (or 1 cup
    frozen corn, thawed)
1 teaspoon salt
2 tablespoons unsalted butter or bacon fat
3 eggs
1 cup buttermilk

Preheat the oven to 400 degrees F. and grease
a 9-inch cast-iron skillet or a 1 1/2-quart
baking dish.

Bring the water to a boil in a 2-quart
saucepan over high heat. Slowly pour in the
cornmeal, stirring well, reduce heat to medium
and cook for 2 minutes. Remove from the
heat. Add the corn kernels, salt and butter and
mix.

In a small bowl, beat the eggs and buttermilk together, then pour into the cornmeal
mixture. Beat with a wire whisk for 1 minute,
or until smooth. Spoon the batter into the
baking dish and bake for 35 to 40 minutes, or
until an inserted knife comes out clean and
the top is nicely browned. *Serves 4 to 6*

Hushpuppies

*Traditionally an accompaniment for fried
fish, these small savory cornmeal "doughnuts"
go with nearly everything. Try serving
them with fresh tomato salsa.*

1/2 cup fine yellow or white cornmeal
1/2 cup all-purpose unbleached flour
1 teaspoon salt, plus more to taste
Large pinch of cayenne
1 teaspoon baking powder
1/2 cup finely chopped green onion
1/2 cup milk
1 egg
1 cup vegetable oil, for frying
Freshly ground black pepper, to taste

In a large mixing bowl, stir together the cornmeal, flour, salt, cayenne and baking powder.
Make a well in this mixture, then add the green
onion, milk and egg. Gradually incorporate the
wet ingredients into the dry, using a wooden
spoon. Beat well with the wooden spoon for 2
minutes longer.

Pour the oil into a large, deep-sided skillet
to a depth of approximately 1/2 inch. Heat the
oil over medium-high heat until almost smoking. Carefully spoon the batter, a tablespoonful
at a time, into the hot oil until the skillet is full
but not crowded with the hushpuppies. Cook,
in batches, approximately 1 minute to a side, or
until golden brown. Drain on paper towels.
Sprinkle with salt and pepper and serve immediately. *Serves 4 to 6*

Back to front: Hushpuppies, a variation of Skillet Corn Bread (recipe p. 48) and Spoon Bread

Skillet Corn Bread

*Although this corn bread can be baked in a pie pan or other baking dish, baking it
in a cast-iron skillet gives it a better crust. The sugar is optional—it is generally frowned upon
by Southerners, and deleting it shows off the natural corn sweetness.*

2 tablespoons vegetable oil or bacon grease
3/4 cup fine yellow cornmeal
1 cup all-purpose unbleached flour
4 tablespoons granulated sugar (optional)
2 teaspoons baking powder

1/2 teaspoon salt
1 egg
2 tablespoons unsalted butter, melted
1 cup buttermilk

Preheat the oven to 425 degrees F.

Pour the oil into a 9-inch cast-iron skillet and place it in the hot oven.

In a large mixing bowl, combine the cornmeal, flour, sugar (if using), baking powder and salt. Make a well in this mixture and add the egg, butter and buttermilk. Gradually incorporate the wet ingredients into the dry, using a wooden spoon or a whisk, then continue to beat for 2 minutes.

Pour the batter carefully into the heated skillet and bake for 20 minutes, or until an inserted knife comes out clean and the top is golden brown. *Serves 4 to 6*

Variation: To use this batter for corn sticks, grease the corn stick molds and put in the preheated oven. Fill the molds approximately two-thirds full and bake for 15 minutes.

Note: Day-old leftover corn bread can be used to make stuffing (see recipe p. 70), or frozen for future use.

Vegetable Fritters

These cornmeal-battered fritters can accompany any number of things: roast beef, swordfish kabobs or spicy grilled chicken breasts. Experiment with other vegetables, such as eggplant, beets or sweet peppers.

Fritter Batter:
1/2 cup all-purpose unbleached flour
3 tablespoons fine yellow cornmeal
1/2 teaspoon baking powder
1/2 teaspoon salt
1 cup milk
2 eggs, separated

2 cups vegetable oil, or as needed, for frying
Kernels from 3 large ears sweet corn (or 1 1/2 cups frozen corn, thawed)

1 cup all-purpose unbleached flour
1 teaspoon salt
Pinch of cayenne
1 red onion, peeled and sliced into 1/4-inch rings
2 cups spinach leaves, washed and drained
Salt and freshly ground black pepper, to taste
2 tablespoons finely chopped Italian parsley, for garnish
2 or 3 lemons, cut into sixths, for garnish

Preheat oven to 250 degrees F.

Prepare the fritter batter: In a large mixing bowl, stir together the flour, cornmeal, baking powder and salt. Make a well in this mixture. Add the milk and egg yolks and beat well with a wooden spoon or whisk for 2 minutes.

In a separate bowl, beat the egg whites until stiff. Add one-third of the beaten whites to the batter and stir them in. Then, using a rubber spatula, fold the rest of the whites gently into the batter.

Pour the oil into a large, deep-sided skillet to a depth of 1/2 inch. Heat the oil over medium-high heat until almost smoking.

Put the corn kernels into a small mixing bowl and coat them well with some of the batter. Slip nuggets of the corn mixture, one tablespoonful at a time, into the hot oil. Fry, in batches, for approximately 1 minute per side,

turning once, or until golden brown. Drain on paper towels and keep warm in the oven.

In a small bowl, combine the flour, salt and cayenne. Dip the onion rings into the seasoned flour, then into the fritter batter, coating them well. Slip the rings into the hot oil, being careful not to crowd them. Fry, in batches, for approximately 2 minutes, turning once, until crisp and golden. Drain on paper towels and keep warm in the oven.

Dip the spinach leaves into the seasoned flour, then into the fritter batter, coating well. Slip the individual leaves into the hot oil. Fry, in batches, for approximately 2 minutes, turning once. Drain on paper towels.

To serve, arrange the fritters on a large platter. Sprinkle with salt, pepper and parsley and garnish with lemon wedges. Serve immediately. *Serves 4 to 6*

"Improved" Creamed Corn

Creamed corn is no longer a bland puddle on the plate. Try this with chicken-fried steak or grilled halibut. Things have improved, haven't they?

2 tablespoons unsalted butter
1 yellow onion, very finely diced
Salt, to taste
Kernels from 4 large ears sweet corn (or 2 cups frozen corn, thawed)
1 teaspoon cumin seed
1 red jalapeño pepper, seeds and veins removed, then very finely chopped

1 green jalapeño pepper, seeds and veins removed, then very finely chopped
1 cup crème fraîche or heavy cream
Freshly ground black pepper, to taste
Juice of 1 large lime
1 tablespoon very thinly sliced chives
1/4 cup loosely packed cilantro sprigs

In a 10-inch sauté pan over low heat, melt the butter. Add the onion and increase the heat to medium. Salt lightly and cook, stirring gently, for 4 to 5 minutes until the onion is completely soft and translucent. Add the corn kernels and cook for 1 minute to warm them through.

In a small dry pan over medium heat, toast the cumin seed until slightly browned and aromatic. Grind in an electric spice mill or with a mortar and pestle to a fine powder. Add to the corn along with the jalapeños and crème fraîche, stir well and simmer for 2 minutes over low heat. Season to taste with salt and pepper, add the lime juice and stir once more.

To serve, transfer the corn to a wide, shallow bowl. Garnish with the chives and cilantro sprigs. *Serves 4*

New England Scalloped Corn

My New England friend says everything is scalloped in New England, even the curtains. This old-fashioned recipe makes everyone feel at home—no matter where they are from. Bring on the pot roast!

5 tablespoons unsalted butter
1 small yellow onion, very finely diced
1 small green bell pepper, very finely diced
Salt, to taste
3 tablespoons all-purpose unbleached flour
Freshly ground black pepper, to taste
1/4 teaspoon paprika

Large pinch of cayenne
1 1/2 cups half-and-half
Kernels from 4 large ears sweet corn (or 2 cups frozen corn, thawed)
2 egg yolks
1/2 cup fresh bread crumbs

Preheat the oven to 375 degrees F.

In a 10-inch skillet over low heat, melt 3 tablespoons of the butter. Add the onion, bell pepper and a little salt. Increase the heat to medium and cook the vegetables without letting them color, stirring occasionally, for approximately 3 minutes. Sprinkle with the flour and season generously with salt and pepper. Add the paprika and cayenne, stirring with a wooden spoon until the flour and seasoning are well incorporated. Gradually add the half-and-half, stirring well as the sauce begins to thicken

to discourage lumps from forming. Lower the heat and simmer for 2 minutes. Remove from the heat and add the corn kernels.

In a small bowl, beat the egg yolks and add to the corn mixture, stirring well. Taste for salt and pepper and adjust as necessary.

Butter a 1 1/2-quart casserole or baking dish. Pour the mixture into the dish and top evenly with the bread crumbs. Dot with the remaining butter. Bake for 30 minutes until nicely browned and bubbly. Serve directly from the baking dish at the table. *Serves 4 to 6*

Corn and Potato Gratin with Thyme and Sage

The French would be shocked to find corn in this dish, which is based on the
classic gratin dauphinois. Although unconventional, the flavors are deep and satisfying.
Serve it with boiled ham or smoked pork chops.

3 tablespoons unsalted butter
2 pounds russet potatoes, peeled and sliced
1/16 inch thick
Salt and freshly ground black pepper, to taste
1 tablespoon roughly chopped fresh sage

1 tablespoon whole fresh thyme leaves
6 cloves garlic, peeled and thinly sliced
Kernels from 3 ears sweet corn (or 1 1/2 cups
frozen corn, thawed)
2 to 3 cups heavy cream

Preheat the oven to 350 degrees F.

Using 1 tablespoon or so of the butter, thickly butter a 2-quart baking dish, preferably an oval gratin dish with 2-inch sides. Make a layer of overlapping potato slices on the bottom of the dish. Sprinkle lightly with salt, pepper, sage, thyme and garlic. Scatter a handful of corn kernels over the potatoes. Drizzle 3 tablespoons of cream over the layer. Continue layering in this fashion until all the potatoes and corn have been used. Pour 2 cups of cream over the top, then push down on the potatoes with a wooden spoon to help distribute the cream evenly. The cream should just barely cover the potatoes. Add more cream if necessary. Cut the remaining butter in small pieces and dot evenly over the surface.

Cover the dish tightly with foil and bake for 45 minutes. Uncover and bake 15 to 20 minutes longer until the top is golden and the potatoes are fork-tender. *Serves 6*

Native American Stew with Corn, Beans and Squash

Conversations with a Native American co-worker provided the inspiration for this dish. When I asked Walter what his family did with corn, his first response was that it was used in prayer. A while later, he told me some ways it could be cooked. Serve this vegetable stew with roast lamb or rabbit.

2 cups Anasazi beans★
2 cups pinto beans
6 dried red chiles, such as ancho, New Mexico Red
    or chili caribe
3 cups water
2 tablespoons vegetable oil
1 large yellow onion, cut into medium dice
Salt, to taste
1 head garlic

1 pound summer squash, cut into medium dice
2 large tomatoes, peeled, seeded and cut into
    medium dice
Kernels from 4 ears Black Aztec or Navajo
    Blue corn★
Freshly ground black pepper, to taste
8 squash blossoms, cut into 1/8-inch strips
1 teaspoon fresh oregano, preferably Mexican
1 tablespoon fresh mint, preferably wild

Place the Anasazi beans in a medium-sized saucepan and add water to cover. Bring to a boil over high heat, lower the heat to maintain a simmer and cook for 1 hour, or until tender. Repeat this procedure with the pinto beans. (Cook the different beans simultaneously, but separately.) Drain and set aside.

In a dry skillet, toast the chiles over medium heat until slightly puffed and aromatic. Split them with a sharp knife and remove the seeds, veins and stems. Place the chiles in a 1-quart saucepan over high heat, add the water and boil for 5 minutes. In a blender, purée the chiles with their cooking liquid. Set aside.

In a Dutch oven or earthenware casserole, heat the oil over medium heat. Add the onion, salt lightly and cook for 3 minutes, allowing the onion to brown slightly. Separate the garlic into cloves, but do not peel, and add to the pot. Pour in the puréed chiles. Stir with a wooden spoon and cook for approximately 2 minutes, or until some of the liquid has evaporated.

Add the summer squash, tomato, corn and beans. Season generously with salt and pepper. Add a little water if the mixture looks too dry. Reduce the heat and simmer, uncovered, for 30 minutes, stirring occasionally. Taste and add salt, if necessary. Add the squash blossoms.

In a dry skillet over medium heat, toast the oregano. Add to the stew and stir well. Coarsely chop the mint, scatter over the stew and serve.
Serves 6 to 8

★ *Anasazi beans are available in many gourmet shops, but any bean, from great white Northern beans to kidney beans, could substitute. It may be difficult to find Black Aztec and Navajo Blue corn unless you grow your own. Substitute any variety of sweet corn or 2 cups frozen corn, thawed.*

Basic Polenta

Polenta existed in Italy before the arrival of corn, made from such cereals as barley and chestnuts.
But now cornmeal polenta is a staple in northern Italy and parts of southern France. If you have a taste
for American cornmeal mush, you'll love polenta. It can be served warm and soft, in a bowl, topped
with a little butter and cheese, or allowed to firm up, then sliced and grilled.

4 cups water
1 teaspoon salt

1 cup yellow coarse cornmeal
2 tablespoons unsalted butter

Bring the water to a boil in a 2-quart heavy-bottomed saucepan over high heat. Add the salt. Slowly pour in the cornmeal, stirring well with a wire whisk. When the water returns to the boil and the polenta begins to thicken, turn the heat to low. Continue to stir every 2 minutes or so, uncovered, for 30 minutes until the grain has swelled. Turn off the heat. Let the polenta rest for 10 minutes, then whisk in the butter. Serve immediately or keep warm over a double boiler. *Serves 4*

For Firm Polenta:
Pour the cooked, still-warm polenta into a baking dish or platter, spreading with a spatula to a thickness of 3/4 inch. Allow to cool at room temperature. Cover and refrigerate for at least 1 hour before using. Firm polenta can be baked, fried or grilled. It will keep for 2 to 3 days in the refrigerator.

Clockwise from the back: Grilled Polenta with
Summer Vegetables (recipe p. 63), Soft Polenta with
Wild Mushroom Ragout (recipe p. 62) and Polenta Torta
with Ricotta and Basil Pesto (recipe p. 64)

Soft Polenta with Wild Mushroom Ragout

Soft polenta is the perfect foil for the deep flavor of this wild mushroom stew.
In summer, try a lighter vegetable stew of eggplant, tomatoes and peppers. A hearty
dish of braised lamb shanks would be perfect with soft polenta, too.

1 recipe soft Basic Polenta (recipe p. 61)
1 pound mixed wild mushrooms (such as chanterelles,
    boletus and black trumpets), or a mixture of button
    mushrooms, shiitakes and oyster mushrooms
1 large yellow onion, finely diced
3 tablespoons extra virgin olive oil
3 to 4 cloves garlic, finely chopped
1/2 cup peeled chopped tomato, fresh or canned
1/2 teaspoon finely chopped fresh thyme

1/2 teaspoon finely chopped fresh sage
1/2 teaspoon finely chopped fresh rosemary
1/4 teaspoon red pepper flakes (optional)
Salt and freshly ground black pepper, to taste
1 1/2 cups unsalted chicken stock, homemade
    or canned, heated
2 tablespoons unsalted butter
2 tablespoons coarsely chopped fresh Italian parsley

Prepare the soft polenta.

Slice or roughly chop the mushrooms approximately 1/8 inch thick. Set aside.

In a 10-inch sauté pan, cook the onion in 2 tablespoons of the oil over medium heat for approximately 2 minutes, letting it brown. Increase the heat to high and add the mushrooms and the remaining 1 tablespoon of oil. Cook for 1 minute, stirring with a wooden spoon and shaking the pan, until the onion and mushrooms are well coated with oil and slightly caramelized.

Reduce the heat to medium and add the garlic, tomato, herbs and red pepper flakes. Season liberally with salt and pepper. Stir to distribute everything evenly. After the tomato liquid has evaporated a little, add the chicken stock and, stirring occasionally, cook for approximately 3 minutes, or until it has reduced by half. Taste and add salt, if necessary. Swirl in the butter and remove from the heat.

To serve, pour the polenta into a large oval platter. Spoon the ragout around the edge. Sprinkle the parsley over the ragout, leaving a vast expanse of golden polenta. *Serves 4 to 6*

Grilled Polenta with Summer Vegetables

Make certain the grill is well oiled, otherwise the
polenta will stick. The polenta's exterior should be crisp and well browned.

1 recipe firm Basic Polenta (recipe p.61)
1/2 cup light olive oil, for brushing
1 large eggplant
4 medium zucchini, yellow and green
1 red onion

4 small tomatoes, ripe but firm
Salt and freshly ground black pepper, to taste
3 tablespoons fruity extra virgin olive oil
1/4 cup loosely packed green basil
1/4 cup loosely packed purple basil (optional)

Prepare the firm polenta, refrigerating it for at least an hour. Prepare a charcoal grill or preheat the broiler. Invert the polenta onto a cutting board and cut it into 3-inch triangles. Brush both top and bottom surfaces with olive oil and grill for 3 minutes on each side. Transfer to a large platter and cover loosely with foil.

Cut the eggplant and zucchini lengthwise into slices 1/2 inch thick. Peel the onion and cut crosswise into slices 1/2 inch thick. Cut the tomatoes in half. Brush all the vegetables on both sides with the light olive oil and season with salt and pepper to taste. Grill the vegetables, in batches, for 2 minutes on each side, or until nicely caramelized but still al dente.

When all the vegetables are grilled, cut them into rough, random shapes and arrange them around the polenta. Drizzle with the extra virgin olive oil and garnish with torn basil leaves. *Serves 4 to 6*

Polenta Torta with Ricotta and Basil Pesto

This dish is prepared exactly like lasagne, but uses polenta instead of pasta. It is excellent with grilled veal chops or roasted chicken, but is equally good on its own as a luncheon dish.

*1 recipe soft Basic Polenta, prepared with 5 cups
    water instead of 4 (recipe p. 61)*
Salt and freshly ground black pepper, to taste
3 tablespoons unsalted butter

Basil Pesto:
2 cups loosely packed fresh basil leaves
1 cup loosely packed Italian parsley

4 to 5 cloves garlic, finely chopped
1/2 cup light olive oil
1/2 cup freshly grated Parmesan cheese
1/2 cup freshly grated Romano cheese

One 15-ounce container ricotta cheese

Preheat the oven to 375 degrees F.

Prepare the polenta. When it is done, season it liberally with salt and pepper and keep warm in a double boiler.

Using half of the butter, thickly butter a 2-quart baking dish, preferably a low earthenware dish with 2-inch sides. Set aside.

To make the pesto, in a food processor fitted with the metal blade, purée the basil, parsley and garlic with a little salt. Scrape down the sides with a rubber spatula. With the motor running, add the oil in a thin stream. Process until smooth. Transfer the purée to a small mixing bowl. In another small bowl, combine the Parmesan and Romano. Add 1/2 cup of the cheese mixture to the pesto. Season with salt and pepper to taste and mix well.

To assemble the torta, ladle one-third of the soft polenta evenly into the prepared baking dish. Spread half the pesto over the polenta and dot with half of the ricotta. Sprinkle the ricotta with one-third of the remaining grated cheese. Now ladle on another layer of polenta. Spread the remaining pesto on top and dot with the remaining ricotta. Sprinkle with half the remaining cheese. Add the final layer of polenta, sprinkle with the last of the cheese and dot with the remaining butter.

Place the dish on a baking sheet and bake, uncovered, for 40 minutes, or until the top is browned and bubbly. *Serves 6*

Spontaneous Succotash

It seems everyone remembers pushing bad cafeteria succotash to the side of the plate. But succotash can be wonderful! Alter this recipe according to what is on hand, or to suit your whims, making sure all the vegetables are cut to a uniform size. The only two constants should be good corn and some kind of bean—but do try to find some of the newly rediscovered fresh summer shelling beans.

1/2 pound fresh lima beans, cranberry beans
    or black-eyed peas★
2 garlic cloves, unpeeled
1 small carrot, peeled
1/2 bay leaf
Salt, to taste
2 tablespoons light olive oil
1 large yellow onion, finely diced
1/4 teaspoon red pepper flakes
2 cloves garlic, finely chopped
1 red bell pepper, finely diced
1 yellow bell pepper, finely diced
1 green zucchini, finely diced

1 yellow zucchini, finely diced
Kernels from 4 large ears sweet corn (or 2 cups
    frozen corn, thawed)
1/2 pound fresh green beans,
    sliced into 1/4-inch-long rounds
1 large ripe red or yellow tomato, peeled, seeded
    and finely diced
1 teaspoon finely chopped fresh thyme
1 teaspoon finely chopped fresh sage
Freshly ground black pepper, to taste
2 tablespoons unsalted butter
1 tablespoon finely chopped Italian parsley
1 tablespoon finely chopped fresh basil

Place the fresh lima beans or other shelling beans in a large pot and add water to cover. Add the garlic cloves, carrot and bay leaf. Over high heat, bring to a boil. Reduce heat to a simmer and cook for 20 to 30 minutes until the beans are tender. Salt to taste and set aside.

In a 3 1/2-quart enamelware pot or Dutch oven, warm the oil over medium heat. Add the onion, salt lightly and cook for approximately 3 minutes until soft and translucent but not browned. Add the red pepper flakes, chopped garlic and bell peppers, and stir well. Cook for 2 minutes, or until the peppers have softened slightly, then add the zucchini. Add a little more salt to help draw some liquid from the zucchini.

Continue cooking for approximately 1 minute, then add the corn and green beans. Cook for 1 minute longer, or until heated through, and add the lima beans, tomato, thyme and sage. Season with pepper and add more salt, if necessary. The vegetables should all be just done—neither too soft nor too crunchy. Swirl in the butter, garnish with parsley and basil and serve immediately. *Serves 4 to 6*

★*Note:* You can substitute thawed frozen baby lima beans or green peas, if necessary. Simply omit the cooking step and add to the succotash as described above.

Baked Saffron Rice with Corn, Onions, Garlic and Peppers

This paella-like baked rice with roasted vegetables is perfect for a casual dinner party. It reheats well, but is delicious served in the Spanish style, at room temperature.

4 large ears sweet corn (or 2 cups frozen corn,
    thawed)
Light olive oil, for brushing corn
2 red bell peppers
2 large red onions
2 heads garlic
Salt and freshly ground black pepper, to taste
3 tablespoons extra virgin olive oil

1 large yellow onion, finely diced
3 cups short-grain white rice
6 cups unsalted vegetable or chicken stock, homemade
    or canned, heated
1/2 teaspoon Spanish saffron, crumbled
Pinch of cayenne
1 tablespoon whole fresh thyme leaves

Preheat the broiler.

Shuck the corn, oil it lightly and roast under the broiler for 10 minutes, turning occasionally, until it colors nicely. Let cool, then using a sharp knife, slice the kernels from the cob and set aside. (If using frozen corn, roast the kernels in a pie pan under the broiler for approximately 5 minutes.)

Roast the peppers under the broiler, turning frequently, for approximately 5 minutes until the skins blacken and blister. Put the peppers in a paper bag and close the bag or place under a towel for 5 minutes to steam, then carefully scrape off the charred skin and seeds with a paring knife. Cut the peppers into 1/4-inch dice and set aside.

Set the oven to 350 degrees F. Peel the red onions and cut each into 8 wedges. Separate the garlic cloves, discarding any excess papery skin, but do not peel. Place the red onion and garlic on a sheet of heavy-duty aluminum foil, salt and pepper lightly and drizzle with 1 tablespoon of the olive oil. Tightly seal the foil and bake for 1 hour, or until the onions and garlic are soft. Let cool, then roughly chop the onion. Squeeze the garlic cloves from their skins. Combine the red onion, garlic, corn and peppers. Set aside.

Over medium heat, sauté the diced yellow onion in the remaining olive oil in a 12-inch Spanish clay casserole or a 3-quart enamelware pot. Salt lightly and cook for 3 minutes without browning. Add the rice and cook for 2 minutes, stirring frequently. Add the stock and simmer for 5 minutes. Add the roasted vegetables, saffron, cayenne and thyme. Taste the broth and add salt, if necessary. Simmer 2 minutes more. Put the casserole into the oven and bake, uncovered, for 20 minutes, or until all the liquid is absorbed. Remove from the oven, cover loosely with foil and allow to rest for 10 minutes before serving. *Serves 6 to 8*

White Corn, Green Bean and Summer Chanterelle Sauté

This vegetable sauté would make an excellent light meal with a loaf of good bread. Or serve alongside lamb, beef, chicken or sea bass. Wild golden chanterelle mushrooms from the Pacific Northwest are available most of the summer. They have an affinity for all summer vegetables, but especially for corn.

1 large yellow onion, finely diced
4 tablespoons extra virgin olive oil
Salt, to taste
Kernels from 4 large ears sweet white corn (or 2 cups frozen corn, thawed)
2 quarts water
2 teaspoons salt
1 pound fresh baby green beans
1/2 pound summer chanterelles, (or button or oyster mushrooms) sliced 1/8 inch thick

2 to 3 cloves garlic, finely chopped
2 teaspoons finely chopped fresh thyme
1/4 teaspoon red pepper flakes (optional)
Juice of 1 lemon, or to taste
Freshly ground black pepper, to taste
2 tablespoons finely chopped Italian parsley
1/4 cup loosely packed basil leaves
Lemon slices, for garnish (optional)

In a 10-inch skillet over medium heat, sauté the onion in 2 tablespoons of the oil for 2 to 3 minutes, being careful not to let it get too brown. Salt lightly and cook for 2 minutes, stirring occasionally. Add the corn and continue cooking for another 2 minutes. Remove from heat. With a rubber spatula, transfer the mixture to a shallow bowl and set aside. Do not wash the skillet—you will use it again.

In a medium-sized saucepan over high heat, bring the water to a hard boil. Add the 2 teaspoons salt. Drop in the green beans and cook for 1 minute. Drain the beans in a colander, then spread them out on a baking sheet or platter to cool at room temperature.

Pour the remaining 2 tablespoons of oil into the 10-inch skillet and turn the heat to medium-high. Add the chanterelles, salt lightly and let them brown on one side. With a spatula or tongs, turn the mushrooms and brown them on the other side. Add the onion and corn mixture and mix well. Reduce the heat to medium. Add the blanched beans and mix again, then add the garlic, thyme and red pepper flakes (if using), stirring well to keep the garlic from burning. Taste for salt and add more if necessary. Continue cooking another 2 minutes.

To serve, pile the vegetables informally on a large oval platter. Squeeze lemon juice over the top and season with pepper. Garnish with the parsley and torn basil leaves, and lemon slices, if desired. Serve immediately.
Serves 4 to 6

Fresh Corn and Corn Bread Stuffing

Pairing sweet corn and smoked bacon makes this stuffing satisfying and aromatic. By baking the stuffing separately from the bird, the surface gets browned and crisp.

2 tablespoons unsalted butter, plus more for
    buttering dish
2 large yellow onions, cut into medium dice
Salt, to taste
3 or 4 cloves garlic, thinly sliced
6 slices smoked bacon, cut into 1/4-inch strips
Kernels from 4 large ears sweet corn
    (or 2 cups frozen corn, thawed)

1 cup finely diced celery
1 tablespoon finely chopped fresh sage
1 tablespoon finely chopped fresh thyme
Pinch of cayenne
Freshly ground black pepper, to taste
4 cups cubed day-old corn bread (recipe p. 51)
1 1/2 cups unsalted chicken stock, homemade or
    canned, heated

Preheat the oven to 375 degrees F. Butter a 3-quart baking dish.

In a 10-inch skillet, melt the 2 tablespoons of butter over medium heat. Add the onion and salt lightly. Stirring frequently, cook for approximately 5 minutes until softened and barely colored. Add the garlic and bacon and cook 2 minutes longer.

Transfer the onion mixture to a large mixing bowl. Add the corn, celery, sage, thyme and cayenne. Season generously with salt and pepper and mix well. Crumble the corn bread into the bowl. With a rubber spatula, mix gently. Slowly pour in the chicken stock and mix again. Adjust the seasoning, if necessary.

Spoon the stuffing into the prepared baking dish, cover with foil and bake for 30 minutes. Uncover and bake 15 to 20 minutes more until crisp and browned on top. *Serves 6 to 8*

MAIN COURSES

Fresh corn! It just sounds like summer. Fettuccine with Corn, Squash and Squash Blossoms can be cooked with vegetables straight from the garden. Spicy Sea Scallop Sauté with Baby Corn is an admirable way to beat the heat. And what could be more American or summery than Barbecued King Salmon with Yankee Corn Relish? Try the Blue Corn Chilaquiles, a savory casserole, for a late summer breakfast or as part of a hot buffet meal. For an outdoor feast, prepare the Yucatan Baked Fish in Banana Leaves in a kettle barbecue, but beware—the smell is so enticing that the neighbors will surely drop by.

Corn can find its way into the main course in other seasons, too. You might want to wait until early autumn and the chile harvest for Red Chile Pork Loin with Corn and Green Chile Popovers. Chicken Gumbo with Corn, Yellow Tomatoes and Okra, with its straightforward earthy appeal, would also make a nice autumn dish. Make the Shrimp and Grits whenever you come across fresh Gulf shrimp. And the *posole,* a heart-warming hominy soup, makes a great meal any time of year. In fact, once posole has become part of your repertoire, you can serve it on every festive occasion—your friends will not complain.

None of these dishes are complicated or fancy, but all of them are inviting. Corn always seems to add a satisfying, homey touch.

Spicy Sea Scallop Sauté with Baby Corn, Ginger, Cilantro and Lime

Asian flavors make these sea scallops sing, and fresh, tender baby corn adds an extravagant chorus of its own.

2 tablespoons peanut oil
1 pound sea scallops, cleaned and lightly salted
20 ears fresh baby corn or canned baby corn
1 tablespoon finely chopped fresh ginger
3 to 4 cloves garlic, finely chopped

1/2 teaspoon red pepper flakes
1/2 teaspoon sesame oil
Salt and freshly ground black pepper, to taste
1 large lime, halved
1/2 cup cilantro sprigs

In a 10-inch sauté pan, heat the oil over high heat. When the oil is nearly smoking, slip in the sea scallops in one layer. Reduce the heat to medium and cook for approximately 2 minutes until the scallops brown well on one side, then turn with tongs and brown the other side. Remove them from the pan and set aside.

Add the baby corn. Shake the pan to coat the corn with the pan juices, then add the ginger, garlic, red pepper flakes, sesame oil and salt and pepper to taste. Cook for 1 minute. Return the scallops to the pan and toss well.

To serve, squeeze the lime halves over the top of the sauté and divide among 4 warmed dinner plates. Garnish with cilantro sprigs.
Serves 4

Shrimp and Grits

*Grits, made from ground hominy (hulled dried corn), are the South's answer
to polenta. The secret to preparing them, according to an outspoken Southern friend, is to cook
them for at least an hour and to let them stick to the bottom of the pot.*

Grits:
4 cups water
2 tablespoons unsalted butter
1 teaspoon salt
1 cup hominy grits
2 to 3 cups milk

2 tablespoons light olive oil
1 large yellow onion, finely diced
Salt, to taste

1 green bell pepper, finely diced
2 tablespoons all-purpose unbleached flour
2 large tomatoes, peeled, seeded and coarsely diced
Freshly ground black pepper, to taste
2 teaspoons paprika
Large pinch of cayenne
2 cups unsalted chicken stock, homemade or canned
*1 1/2 pounds fresh Gulf shrimp, peeled
    and deveined*

In a 2-quart saucepan over high heat, bring the water to a boil. Add the butter and salt and slowly pour in the grits. Bring the water back to a boil, stirring well as the grits thicken. Reduce heat to a simmer. Cook for at least an hour, every 10 minutes adding approximately half a cup of milk and stirring, until the grits are the consistency of thin mashed potatoes. Remove from heat and cover to keep warm.

In a 10-inch skillet, heat the oil. Add the onion, salt lightly and cook 3 minutes over medium heat without browning. Add the bell pepper and continue cooking until the vegetables brown slightly. Sprinkle in the flour, stirring with a wooden spoon. Add the tomato and season liberally with salt and black pepper. Add the paprika, cayenne and chicken stock. Reduce heat to low and simmer for 5 minutes. Check the sauce for seasoning and adjust if necessary. Slip in the shrimp and cover the pan. They should be done in 2 minutes.

To serve, dish a big spoonful of grits and a big spoonful of shrimp with plenty of sauce onto each plate. *Serves 4 to 6*

Barbecued King Salmon with Yankee Corn Relish and Grilled Green Onions

In the summer, king salmon runs the entire length of the Pacific Coast. It feeds on shrimp, which gives the flesh a brilliant red color and an amazing sweetness. Paired with a traditional corn relish and grilled green onions, it puts foreign fare to shame. This dish is also very good at room temperature. Serve it with freshly dug new potatoes.

Yankee Corn Relish:
1 quart cider vinegar
4 large ears sweet corn, boiled (see p. 43) and
  kernels removed (or 2 cups frozen corn, thawed)
1 cup finely diced celery
1 cup finely diced green cabbage
1 cup finely diced red bell pepper
1 cup finely diced yellow bell pepper
1 cup peeled, seeded cucumber, finely diced
1/2 teaspoon dry mustard
1/4 teaspoon cayenne

1/2 teaspoon turmeric
2 tablespoons granulated sugar
Salt, to taste

2 bunches green onions
4 king salmon steaks, 6 ounces each
4 tablespoons light olive oil
Salt and freshly ground black pepper, to taste
1 teaspoon finely chopped fresh dill
1 teaspoon finely chopped fresh parsley
1 teaspoon finely chopped fresh chives

In a 4-quart stainless steel or enamelware pot, bring the vinegar to a boil. Add the remaining relish ingredients and simmer for 2 minutes. Strain, saving both vegetables and liquid. Allow to cool to room temperature, then recombine. This relish can be made several days in advance and kept covered in the refrigerator.

Prepare a bed of coals or preheat the broiler. Rinse the green onions clean. Trim the ends slightly, but leave them whole. Drizzle the salmon and green onions with olive oil and season with salt and pepper. Grill the salmon for 3 minutes per side and the green onions for 1 minute per side.

To serve, spoon 1 tablespoon of relish over the fish, surround with grilled green onions and scatter the dill, parsley and chives across the top. *Serves 4*

Yucatan Baked Fish in Banana Leaves with Corn, Rice and Black Beans

If you're not lucky enough to have a banana tree in your yard, you can find frozen banana leaves from the Philippines at many ethnic markets. They're good for wrapping tamales and fish, and they also make great disposable plates. This fish can also be baked in a covered kettle barbecue. The aroma is intoxicating.

2 cups black beans
2 garlic cloves, unpeeled
1/2 bay leaf
Salt, to taste
4 slices (6 ounces each) white sea bass
Freshly ground black pepper, to taste
4 teaspoons achiote paste (available in Mexican grocery stores)
Juice of 1/2 orange
Banana leaves, parchment paper or aluminum foil
Kernels from 4 large ears sweet corn (or 2 cups frozen corn, thawed)

1 cup long-grain white rice
1 1/2 cups water
1/2 teaspoon salt
1 yellow tomato, finely diced
1 jalapeño pepper, very finely chopped
Juice of 1 lime
1/2 cup red onion, finely diced
1 bunch cilantro, for garnish
12 small radishes, for garnish
1 orange, sliced, for garnish
1 lime, cut into wedges, for garnish

Place the black beans in a medium-sized saucepan, add water to cover and bring to a boil over high heat. Reduce the heat to simmer and add the garlic cloves and the bay leaf. Simmer for 1 hour, or until tender. Salt to taste and set aside.

Preheat the oven to 450 degrees F.

Season the sea bass lightly with salt and pepper. In a cup, dissolve the achiote paste in the orange juice and smear it over the fish. Cut the banana leaves into 8-inch squares and put them in the oven for 30 seconds, or until they become pliable (omit this step if using parchment or foil). Lay a slice of fish on a leaf, top with 1/2 cup of corn kernels, then fold the package closed, securing with a toothpick.

Meanwhile, in a 1-quart saucepan or rice steamer over high heat, bring the rice, water and salt to a boil. Lower the heat to a simmer and cook, covered, for 15 minutes. Remove from the heat, cover the pot with a dish towel and let the rice sit for 10 minutes. Fluff with a fork before serving.

In a small bowl, toss the black beans with the yellow tomato, jalapeño, lime juice, red onion and a little salt.

Place the fish packages on a baking sheet and bake for 10 minutes, or until the fish flakes easily but is still moist.

Serve the fish in its package, accompanied by the steamed rice and black beans. Garnish with sprigs of cilantro, the radishes, orange slices and lime wedges. *Serves 4*

Posole

Posole (or pozole) is a heart-warming hominy soup with as many versions as there are cooks. Sold as late-night street food in Mexico, it is also a standard item on most menus in northern New Mexico restaurants. It makes a great dinner soup for friends. Some people like to serve the hominy without the broth as a side dish.

2 large yellow onions, peeled and cut into 1-inch dice
1 head garlic
3 cups dried hominy
1 smoked ham hock
3 pounds meaty pork ribs
3 tablespoons Chimayo chile powder★
1 tablespoon cumin seed
12 cups water
Salt, to taste

Garnishes:
2 tablespoons oregano, toasted in a dry skillet
1 finely diced red onion
1 avocado, sliced
3 limes, cut in small wedges
1 cup cilantro, coarsely chopped
3 coarsely chopped jalapeño peppers
Warm tortillas, for accompaniment

Combine the onion, garlic, hominy, ham hock, ribs, chile powder, cumin seed and water in a large soup pot. Bring to a boil, then reduce heat to low, skimming off any froth that rises to the top. Simmer, uncovered, for 3 to 3 1/2 hours until the pork meat is falling off the bone. Skim off any fat that rises to the surface. Taste the broth and add salt if necessary.

To serve, arrange the garnishes in little dishes so that guests can help themselves. Ladle the posole into deep bowls and serve accompanied by warm tortillas. *Serves 4 to 6*

★Note: You can find the Chimayo chile powder in a Mexican grocery store or any supermarket in the Southwest. Otherwise, substitute 3 tablespoons paprika and 1/4 teaspoon cayenne or any medium-ground, spicy red chile.

Blue Corn Chilaquiles with White Corn and Poblano Chiles

Once you make this savory tortilla casserole, you'll wonder how you lived without it. If blue corn tortillas are not available, use the best corn tortillas you can find; do not substitute flour tortillas. Do attempt to find poblano chiles (sometimes mistakenly called pasilla chiles). Otherwise use fresh New Mexico green or Anaheim chiles.

4 poblano chiles
12 blue corn tortillas
1 cup vegetable oil, for frying
2 teaspoons cumin seed
1 pound yellow tomatoes
1 small onion
2 cloves garlic
2 tablespoons lard or olive oil

Pinch of cayenne
Salt and freshly ground black pepper, to taste
4 large ears sweet white corn, boiled (see p. 43) and
    kernels removed (or 2 cups frozen corn, thawed)
4 ounces Monterey Jack cheese, grated
4 ounces queso fresco★ or mild feta cheese, for garnish
Cilantro sprigs, for garnish

Preheat the broiler.

Roast the poblano chiles under the broiler, turning frequently, for approximately 5 minutes until the skins blacken and blister. Put the peppers in a paper bag and close the bag or place under a towel for 5 minutes to steam, then carefully scrape off the charred skin and seeds with a paring knife. Set aside.

Preheat the oven to 350 degrees F. Lightly oil a wide earthenware casserole or a Pyrex baking dish.

Cut the tortillas into 1-inch strips. Heat the vegetable oil in a deep-sided skillet over medium heat until almost smoking. Fry the tortilla strips until barely crisp; do not let them color. Drain on paper towels. Strain and save the oil for another use.

In a dry skillet over medium heat, toast the cumin seed until lightly browned and aromatic. Grind in an electric spice mill or with a mortar and pestle. Set aside.

Put the yellow tomato, onion and garlic in the blender and process until smooth. In a 10-inch skillet over medium heat, heat the lard until almost smoking, then add the tomato mixture. Cook, stirring occasionally, for 5 minutes. Season with the toasted cumin and the cayenne and add salt and pepper to taste.

Place the tortilla strips in a large mixing bowl. Pour the tomato sauce over them, tossing with 2 wooden spoons. Cut the poblanos into 1/4-inch ribbons. Begin layering ingredients into the casserole dish: tortilla strips, corn, poblanos and Monterey Jack cheese. Continue layering until all the ingredients are used, finishing with a layer of tortilla strips.

Bake for 40 minutes, or until bubbling, crisp and golden. Garnish with crumbled *queso fresco* and cilantro. Allow to cool 5 minutes before serving. *Serves 4 to 6*

★ *Note:* Queso fresco is a soft, fresh Mexican cheese. It can be found in Mexican groceries.

Red Chile Pork Loin with Corn and Green Chile Popovers

In early autumn the air in Santa Fe is filled with the smell of roasting green chiles. In the farmers' market red chile ristras—long strands of local chiles, often hung in doorways and kitchens—make their first appearance. This dish was designed to approximate the giddy feeling we get at that time of year. Serve it with a green salad or sautéed greens.

2 tablespoons cumin seed
1 boneless pork loin roast, approximately 2 pounds
6 cloves garlic, thinly sliced
Salt and freshly ground black pepper, to taste
6 tablespoons powdered red chile, such as ancho
    or Chimayo

Corn and Green Chile Popovers:
2 tablespoons unsalted butter, for buttering tins

2 eggs
1 cup milk
1 tablespoon melted butter
1 cup all-purpose unbleached flour
1/2 teaspoon salt
Kernels from 3 large ears white corn (or 1 1/2 cups
    frozen corn, thawed)
2 to 3 jalapeño peppers, seeded and very
    finely chopped

Preheat the oven to 450 degrees F.

In a dry skillet over medium heat, toast the cumin seed until lightly browned and aromatic. Grind in an electric spice mill or with a mortar and pestle. Set aside.

Make small slits in the pork loin with a sharp paring knife and insert the garlic slices. Season the entire loin liberally with salt and pepper. Rub the loin with the red chile and cumin. (For a more intense flavor, do this several hours ahead and cover and refrigerate the pork. Bring it to room temperature before proceeding.) Roast the pork loin on a rack for approximately 35 minutes, or until a meat thermometer registers 130 degrees F. Remove from the oven and let the roast rest while the popovers are baking. Cover loosely with foil and let rest in a warm place. Do not turn off the oven.

Meanwhile, butter muffin tins or popover pans. In a mixing bowl, with a wire whisk or electric beater, combine the eggs, milk, melted butter, flour and salt. Mix well for approximately 2 minutes until the batter is free of lumps and is the consistency of heavy cream.

In a small bowl, mix together the corn kernels and jalapeños. Fill the muffin tins half full of batter and drop a spoonful of the corn mixture into each. Bake for 15 minutes, then reduce heat to 350 degrees F. and bake 15 minutes longer, or until the popovers are golden brown.

Slice the pork loin, arrange on a large platter and warm in the oven for 2 minutes before serving.

To serve, pass a platter of the sliced pork loin and a basket of the popovers. *Serves 4 to 6*

Chicken Gumbo with Corn, Yellow Tomatoes and Okra

*This hearty gumbo is for big eaters. Supply them with lemonade, mint juleps and
hammocks for a long, lazy meal.*

3 pounds chicken legs, cut in half
1/2 cup vegetable oil
2 large yellow onions, cut into 1-inch dice
1 cup green bell pepper pieces, in 1-inch dice
1 cup yellow bell pepper pieces, in 1-inch dice
1 cup celery pieces, in 1-inch dice
Salt, to taste
1/2 cup all-purpose unbleached flour
*2 pounds yellow tomatoes, peeled, seeded and
    coarsely diced*
1 tablespoon finely chopped garlic
8 cups water
*1/2 pound spicy Louisiana sausage,
    sliced 3/8 inch thick*

1/2 pound okra, sliced 1/8 inch thick
*Kernels from 3 large ears sweet corn (or 1 1/2 cups
    frozen corn, thawed)*
1 tablespoon finely chopped fresh thyme
Salt and freshly ground black pepper, to taste
Cayenne, to taste
2 cups long-grained white rice
1/2 teaspoon salt
3 cups water
3 tablespoons thinly sliced green onions, for garnish
*2 tablespoons finely chopped Italian parsley,
    for garnish*

In a 4-quart Dutch oven or enamelware pot over medium heat, brown the chicken pieces lightly in the oil for approximately 3 to 5 minutes on each side, turning frequently. Remove the chicken and reserve. Add the onion, bell peppers and celery. Salt lightly and cook for 3 minutes. Add the flour, stirring well with a wooden spoon. Continue cooking for 5 or 6 minutes until the flour is quite brown. Add the tomato, garlic and water and bring the mixture to a boil. Return the chicken to the pot and reduce the heat to a simmer.

Cover and cook for 1 hour, or until the chicken is very tender. Add the sausage, okra,

corn and thyme. Cook for another 10 minutes. Skim off any fat that has risen to the surface. Check seasoning and add salt, pepper and cayenne to taste.

Begin the rice 25 minutes before serving. Place the rice, salt and water in a medium-sized saucepan and bring to a boil over high heat. Lower the heat to simmer and cook, covered, for 15 minutes. Remove from heat, cover the pot with a dish towel and let the rice sit for 10 minutes. Fluff with a fork before serving.

To serve, ladle the gumbo into big soup bowls over the rice. Garnish with green onions and parsley. *Serves 6*

Fettuccine with Corn, Squash and Squash Blossoms

If you grow your own corn and squash, this pasta will be divine. Otherwise try to find the fresh vegetables at a farmers' market. Do not be tempted to serve grated cheese with this dish—the flavors are too delicate.

3 quarts water
2 tablespoons extra virgin olive oil
1 large yellow onion, very finely diced
Salt, to taste
1 pound baby summer squash or zucchini,
*   with blossoms*
Kernels from 3 large ears white corn (or 1 1/2 cups
*   frozen corn, thawed)*
1 teaspoon finely chopped fresh thyme

2 to 3 cloves garlic, finely chopped
Freshly ground black pepper, to taste
1/2 cup unsalted chicken stock, heated
1 pound fresh egg fettuccine
2 tablespoons unsalted butter
Juice of 1 lemon
8 large basil leaves, cut into 1/8-inch strips
2 tablespoons finely chopped Italian parsley
1 tablespoon thinly sliced chives

Bring the water to a boil in a large, wide pot.

In a 10-inch sauté pan, heat the oil over medium heat. Add the onion, salt lightly, and cook for 4 to 5 minutes until the onion is soft and barely colored.

Meanwhile, remove the blossoms from the squash and slice them into 1/8-inch strips. Set aside. Slice the squash into 1/8-inch rounds and add to the onions. Sauté for 1 minute, then add the corn, thyme and garlic. Season with salt and pepper to taste. Add the chicken stock, increase the heat to high and continue cooking for 1 minute. Remove from heat.

Salt the boiling water and cook the fettuccine at a rapid boil for 2 minutes, or until the pasta is al dente. Drain the fettuccine in a colander, then return it to the cooking pot. Pour the squash and corn mixture over the pasta and add the blossom strips and the butter. Squeeze lemon juice over the pasta, toss gently and divide among 4 heated bowls. Garnish with basil, parsley and chives. *Serves 4*

METRIC CONVERSIONS

Liquid Weights

U.S. Measurements	Metric Equivalents
1/4 teaspoon	1.23 ml
1/2 teaspoon	2.5 ml
3/4 teaspoon	3.7 ml
1 teaspoon	5 ml
1 dessertspoon	10 ml
1 tablespoon (3 teaspoons)	15 ml
2 tablespoons (1 ounce)	30 ml
1/4 cup	60 ml
1/3 cup	80 ml
1/2 cup	120 ml
2/3 cup	160 ml
3/4 cup	180 ml
1 cup (8 ounces)	240 ml
2 cups (1 pint)	480 ml
3 cups	720 ml
4 cups (1 quart)	1 litre
4 quarts (1 gallon)	3 3/4 litres

Dry Weights

U.S. Measurements	Metric Equivalents
1/4 ounce	7 grams
1/3 ounce	10 grams
1/2 ounce	14 grams
1 ounce	28 grams
1 1/2 ounces	42 grams
1 3/4 ounces	50 grams
2 ounces	57 grams
3 ounces	85 grams
3 1/2 ounces	100 grams
4 ounces (1/4 pound)	114 grams
6 ounces	170 grams
8 ounces (1/2 pound)	227 grams
9 ounces	250 grams
16 ounces (1 pound)	464 grams

Temperatures

Fahrenheit	Celsius (Centigrade)
32°F (water freezes)	0°C
200°F	95°C
212°F (water boils)	100°C
250°F	120°C
275°F	135°C
300°F (slow oven)	150°C
325°F	160°C
350°F (moderate oven)	175°C
375°F	190°C
400°F (hot oven)	205°C
425°F	220°C
450°F (very hot oven)	230°C
475°F	245°C
500°F (extremely hot oven)	260°C

Length

U.S. Measurements	Metric Equivalents
1/8 inch	3 mm
1/4 inch	6 mm
3/8 inch	1 cm
1/2 inch	1.2 cm
3/4 inch	2 cm
1 inch	2.5 cm
1 1/4 inches	3.1 cm
1 1/2 inches	3.7 cm
2 inches	5 cm
3 inches	7.5 cm
4 inches	10 cm
5 inches	12.5 cm

Approximate Equivalents

1 kilo is slightly more than 2 pounds

1 litre is slightly more than 1 quart

1 meter is slightly over 3 feet

1 centimeter is approximately 3/8 inch

INDEX